Waves and Other Poems

A Collection of Fourty Seven Poems

San Lin Tun

ISBN 978-93-5458-449-7

Published in India 2021 by Pencil

Contributors:
Editor: San Lin Tun
Editor: Andrew King
Editor: San Lin Tun
Editor: Andrew King

A brand of
One Point Six Technologies Pvt. Ltd.
123, Building J2, Shram Seva Premises,
Wadala Truck Terminal, Wadala (E)
Mumbai 400037, Maharashtra, INDIA
E connect@thepencilapp.com
W www.thepencilapp.com

Author biography

San Lin Tun (b.1974) is a freelance writer of essays, poetry, short story and novel in Myanmar and English. He authored over ten English books including "Readng a George Orwell Novel in a Myanmar Teashop and Other Essays", "The Enigma of Big Bunny's Arrival and Other Short Stories", "A Shirt and Other Poems", "An English Writer", etc.

His writings appeared in local and international publications such as Asia Literary Review, Borderless, Countercurrent, Kitaab, Mad in Asia Pacific, Mekong Review, Myanmar Times, My Yangon Magazine, Myanmore, New Asian Writing Anthology (NAW), PIX, Ponder Savant, Pure Haiku, South East of Now, Strukturriss and several others.

He is the first prize winner of poetry of Wales National Day in 2015. He holds an M.A (BDh), B.E (Metallurgy), AmPox.3, and Start Writing Fiction. He lives in Yangon with his wife and two sons.

CONTENTS

Books by the same author 14

1. WAVES 15

2. UNTIED EXISTENCE 16

3. WITH OR WITHOUT REASON 17

4. NO MORE BELIEVE IN MYTHS 18

5. A BLANK HEART 19

6. AFTERMATH 20

7. ALGEBRA OF ADVICE 21

8. A BRIGHT LIGHT 22

9. ONLY THEN 23

10. A CHANCE TO CHOOSE 24

11. A TURN 25

12. THE LIGHT 26

13. NATURE 27

14. HOPE 28

15. RESILIENCE 29

16. ADVICE 30

17. COOKIES 31

18. MY LAMP 32

19. FREEDOM 33

20. A NEW FORM OF RELATIONSHIP 34

21. IN EQUAL STATE 35

22. A CHOICE 36

23. A NEW START 37

24. TRUE LOVE 38

25. SILENCE 39

26. A SINCERE WISH 40

27. JOE'S STORY 41

28. NO APPLAUSE, PLEASE 42

29. THE ACT OF WASHIG UP 43

30. TO THE GOAL 44

31. ANIMATION POEM 45

32. FAILURE 46

33. UNTITLED LIFE 47

34. URBAN FEATURES 49

35. RIGHT ANSWER 51

36. MUM'S GIRL 52

37. FEAR OF LOSS 55

38. AN EGOCENTRIC BOSOM OF DESERT 56

39. A REMEDY TO AN EGOCENTRIC BOSOM OF DESRT 57

40. BULLET-1 58

41. BULLET-2 59

42. YANGON CITY 60

43. LONELINESS 62

44. A JUMP 63
45. FEAR-1 64
46. FEAR-2 65
47. TO THE MAN WHO LIVED IN 29TH STREET . 66

Epigraph

I came out alone on my way to my tryst.
But who is this that follows me in the silent dark? --- Rabindranath TAGORE

Preface

ENDORSEMENTS

It's difficult not to be disarmed by San Lin Tun's poetry; his poems are often quirky, philosophical and even gnomic, but always humane. *Waves and Other Poems*displays his considerable development as a poet in a growing list of other writerly achievements. His Poems have the mark of the true poet. ---Joseph Woods, poet and writer

Serene and inviting! San Lin Tuns' poetry brings a sense of peacefulness while engaging with the reader in the wide range of human emotions. He dances with the joyous and the amusing sentiments, creating warm smiles and soft chuckles. He draws attention to the simple things in life that one might have missed. Even when exploring the darker topics such as fear or loss, he writes with ease, making a daunting subject feel natural. He lifts the heaviness and welcomes being human, in all its complications and yet expressed so purely that it doesn't seem complicated at all. The book is a gentle trail of hope led by reminders of the beauty around us and in us. Reading it is like taking a tender walk in nature. It has the safeness of being alone, while feeling connected and heard. It's rejuvenating, meditative, and healing. ---Mia Savant, creator of pondersavant.com

There is a charming simplicity in San Lin's poems but they leave their mark, making you think deeply. San Lin's themes come from life itself, missed chances, the darkness that exists but light that must shine including a beloved's smile that may be a 'lamp for his own life'. His work is almost like a reassurance to hold on, that life will come with pain, with losses, but that we should not fear it at all. ---Jhilmil Breckenridge, poet, writer and activist and author of *Reclamation Song*

"Fetters are left behind", San Lin Tun writes in his poem *Freedom*. "Hovering in the sky, Feel free and independent", the poem continues. These words capture the spirit of his latest book *Waves and Other Poems*. Such a prolific writer, of fact and fiction, personal profiles and cultural histories, this current book expresses a sense of freedom in both words and form. No two poems are alike, and explore the process of writing just as they do the subjects of each poem.

Urban landscapes, personal preferences, reaching goals and dealing with failure, relationships, hopes and even cookies, these are the topics you'll be expected to read about in his eclectic collection of musings. If you find yourself stuck for conversation, or in need of inspiration to write something yourself, pick up this book, turn to any page and just read. ---Andrew King, Lifestyle Editor at The Myanmar Times

Acknowledgements

My sincere thanks go to Joseph Woods, an Irish poet and writer who shows much sympathies and cheerfulness whenever I meet him on literary occasions in Yangon, and wrote an endorsement for the book, Mia Savant, a founder of Ponder Savant who kindly wrote me an endorsement on the book, Jhilmil Breckenridge, poet, writer and activist and author of *Reclamation Song*who showed me keenness when I need a favour for endorsement and Andrew King, Lifestyle Editor at Myanmar Times for his wonderful endorsement. Finally, I would like to express my thanks to my readers who support my writing career. Without their support, this book cannot see the light of day.

Introduction

I write poetry when something stirrs up my mind. It may be a view or a picture or a thought. Then, I try to grasp its essence to compose a poem. Sometimes, a thought flickers in my mind and I have to sit up on bed to write it down, especially when my eyelids are heavy and I am ready to drift into the dreamy world.

I remember from my reading that a surrelist painter holds his key in hand and he waits for his time to sleep. Soon, he feels drowsy and the keys drop from his hand. Hearing the clinging of the keys, he wakes up to memorize the image he has seen in his dreamy state.

My case might be similar to him. If I do not sit up to write down a poem, I will lose it. I think you might experience this when you are trying to write poetry, especially when your muse urges you to write a poem. In my opinion, reading a poem is like looking at an abstract painting or listening to jazz music.

For me, I published my first collection of poetry titled "*A Shirt and Other Poems*" in 2015. Five years later, and after sporadic writing on poetry, I have managed to collect forty seven poems of mine into a book. This book marks another literary milestone for me.

In this collection, you will read some poems are funny, some are about romance, some are about philisophical, some are inspiration, etc. Anyway, I hope you will enjoy reading them.

Books by the same author

The Legendary Heroes of Myanmar
Ancient Myanmar Heroes
Walking Down An Old Literary Road
A Classic Night At Cafe Blues and Other Stories
A Shirt And Other Poems
Reading A George Orwell Novel In A Myanmar Teashop And Other Essays
The Enigma of Big Bunny's Arrival and Other Short Stories
An iSmart Bus Ride And Other Essays
Yangon Street Walker (co-author Keith Lyons)
An English Writer
Learning Alphabets/My Birthday/Flying With Balloon
First Collection of Graphic Poems
Beyond Image (written in Myanmar language)

1. WAVES

Waves form
at sea.

Some reach the shore,
But, some don't.

2. UNTIED EXISTENCE

No bondage
in vacuum.

Unstable,
mind,
drifting,
flowing,
vexation,

It happens.

3. WITH OR WITHOUT REASON

The sun shies
With or without reason.
Rain falls
With or without reason.
Wind blows
With or without reason.
Fire burns
With or without reason.
Man seeks happiness
With or without reason.
I write poems
With or without reason.

4. NO MORE BELIEVE IN MYTHS

No more believe
in myths,
Whatever they says:
"*Good-hearted men*
Will find beautiful girls".

5. A BLANK HEART

Mind,
much free and independent,

No volume at all.
No width and length.

It's not a DVD player
that can be pressed on its pause button.

It's not an open TV set,
It's not dumb too.

Actually,
it's blank.

6. AFTERMATH

I have written poems,
Five of them today.
All I have read,
But, nothing of them brings me
any satisfaction.
So, I tore them apart.
In the shattered,
Among pieces of paper,
A word stands out very clearly.
On it, it says,
"*What?*"

7. ALGEBRA OF ADVICE

Plus your effort,
Minus your negative views,
Multiply your energy,
Divide by your sloth.

8. A BRIGHT LIGHT

If you want to dispel
The darkness,
Not put on the light,
Just open a book.
The book has many lamps
That shine everything and everyone,
And finally lives brighten
Under the bright light.

9. ONLY THEN

Good is good
Bad is bad,
They cannot mingle.
Poverty is not a sin,
Only the exploitation of it is a sin.
Wealth is not a blessing,
Only when it is shared, it is a blessing.

10. A CHANCE TO CHOOSE

A trodden old road,
on seeing,
dust rolling.

An untrodden road,
beseeking,
bushes entangling.

11. A TURN

A fallen fruit!
Running to pick it up with glee,
There is someone
Already, ahead of me.

12. THE LIGHT

A speck of light
That dispels darkness,
Stronger with time,
Brighter than before,
Only then it will totally eradicate darkness,
One will reach the world of light.

13. NATURE

The sun is to shine,
The moon is to adore,
A life to live,
A heart to love.

14. HOPE

A stolen fruit,
Frustrated and despaired he felt,
But, hopeful again,
‘cos he sees it in her hand.

15. RESILIENCE

Put your shirt on,
No matter how hot,
or cold it is.

16. ADVICE

Some say,
Out of sight,
Out of mind.

My advice for you,
Is put your glasses on,
If you don't want to

Lose your mind,
That will make things
More clearly for you.

17. COOKIES

Crunchy,
Munchy,
But trendy.

18. MY LAMP

A bee can produce
Plenty of honey.
A flower can produce
Lots of beauty.
A laughter can enhance
The health of the globe.
As for your smile
It is a lamp
For my whole life.

19. FREEDOM

All fetters are left behind,
Hovering in the sky,
Feel free and independent.

20. A NEW FORM OF RELATIONSHIP

Love should be equal,
No matter what it takes.
One-sided love or unrequited love
Whatever they call brings
No equal emotional sensation.
Sometimes, love is changed
Into a certain condition forces
To change _ agree or disagree.
But, love will remain
As it was, as it is,
And as it will be.

21. IN EQUAL STATE

When you win, I win.
When you lose, I lose.
When you are happy, I am happy.
We are in equal state.
I do not want to feel happy,
When you are unhappy.
You and me are in the same state.

22. A CHOICE

A person has a choice
Want to be good or bad?
When he faces any infavourable condition.
Be good or bad?
It depends on him.
Want to be good?
Then, be good.
Want to be bad?
It's not good for anyone.
But, he has got a choice.

23. A NEW START

He understands he needs
To change it.
He knows he needs a new life
To live again.
Sometimes, life is like that.
He sees things are changing.
He can't control it.
He has no power to keep it still.
Everything is happening in its own way.
He knows that time he needs
A new mind to start it again.

24. TRUE LOVE

I know your love
For me is true.
You love me better than
Anyone else.
        I value it,
        I respect it,
        I cherish it,
        I will always keep it
In my mind and heart.

25. SILENCE

Everything seems silent,
Quiet in its own way.
Even thoughts become freeze,
Words stuck.
Though walking,
Just a walk.
Neither happy nor unhappy.
Silence in heart.

26. A SINCERE WISH

A wish is made sincerely,
May a flower bloom,
May a person be happy,
May everything be fine,
May everyone be free from worries.
May you be free from worries,
Sufferings, in equality, have peace of mind,
Be successful, be loved by one you love,
May you meet and live together
Happily with the one you love truly.

27. JOE'S STORY

Hey, Joe!
Where are you going?
He said, "I don't know."
Where do you come from?
He said, "This one still I don't know."
Where will you go then?
He said, "That one also I don't know."

28. NO APPLAUSE, PLEASE

I sing a song,
when no one is around.

Not fear of criticism,
But fear of applause.

29. THE ACT OF WASHIG UP

My hands become smeared,
Hurriedly I ran and wash them,
As soon as I turn on the tap,
Water's jumping out.
Hastily and happily,
I put my hands under it.
To my surprise,
The water is also unclean
And smeared.

30. TO THE GOAL

Hit it hard,
Kick it straight,
With full strength
and with haste.
Then,
You will score the goal.

31. ANIMATION POEM

A poem animated,
It comes to visualize on screen,
one word, then flickers on,
off-on with another word,
displaying longitudinally.

The first word, *on*
The second word, *off*
The third word, *on*
The fourth word, *off*
The first line is totally shown.

Interrupted by icons,
Flowers, smiling faces, cheering crowds,
So magnificently to behold,
Read it, enjoy it, and embrace it.

32. FAILURE

When he see things unfair,
He knows it's not fair.
Also, he cannot do any justification on it,
    He feels despaired,
    It's not his fault
    He understands it.
He knows sometimes
Things are complicated
In their own ways.
But, he hopes the justification
Comes up for its own cause.
Then, it will lighten up
All things. There will be no
Failure at all.

33. UNTITLED LIFE

What the most important thing will be,
In life for a man; how he will find out and prove;
There will be different opinions, and views,
But, the decisive action will be his due.

Find the way, don't messy with others,
Who want to find glory, fame and eternity;
Being forgetful of the ephemeral nature of things,
The more they attach to them, the more they suffer.

Though they know, they stick to them more,
Hard, solid life they will lead and tread on;
When there is no one around them, solitude, and desperate,
To whom will they tend to when they feel sorrow.

To whom will they share their love when they feel merry,
Needed in life is companions, and friendship;
Living solo or alone is out of question, inconsistency in life,
Life is not meant for that, but for living.

Think about it, then take action,
To share is a must when you live your life;
It is a human value, and pride to share with others,

So, empathy will be recited as a mantra.

Won't let it happen before your eyes,
Which should be wide open, together with your heart;
This is life whether you like it or not, but accept it as it comes,
You will learn and experience a lot to be a matured one.

They said save enough to spend later and secured,
Orient yourself to be a bountiful person;
A good scheme is what we need in life.
Then, life will be in delight with full bright.

34. URBAN FEATURES

Streets and roads become much wider,
Is it needed for people to walk more?

*Walkability?*Traffic jams happen when roads and cars
are not consistent in magnitude.

To seek wealth, and joy, urban migration happens.
Paddy fields are in need of growers, and planters.

It's necessary to walk fast in city,
They suggest crossing roads boldly,

Even at zebra crossings; drivers surely slam their brakes,
What needs is to reach the other side in time.

Buses going back home must be crowded,
Delightfully people can ride and join the band.

It's euphonic to be called urbanites, or city dwellers,
But, take care of pick-pockets when taking buses home.

At bus stops, priority given to man in front to descend,
The queuing is needed as decorum; so, don't hustle when
getting off buses.

In 2030, population will be increased double,
More jobs and more houses will be on the way,

Life is supposed to be a daily activity or struggle,
Think about it, it's so sure that the urban city

Will be adorned more with high condos, and high rise buildings.

35. RIGHT ANSWER

Day or night?
I ask, which one do you like?
Day, of course, I like. That's the answer right.
Hamburger or hot dog?
I ask, which one do you like?
Both of them, of course, I like. That's the answer right.
Brad Pitt or George Clooney?
I ask, whom do you like?
Sometimes Brad Pitt,
Sometimes George Clooney, I like them too much.
East or West?
I ask, which one do you like?
Of course, I like, both. That's the answer right.
You, my lover, me or money?
I ask, which one do you like?
She thought for a while,
Then, give me an answer,
That's so bright, she said,
I love you so much.
That's the answer right.

36. MUM'S GIRL

A little girl is gazing distantly,
Beside her lay garlands of Jasmine,
Which she sells for her living.

The scene becomes blurred.

Neither moving nor standing,
She is just sitting on a bench
With is facing steady flowing Yangon River.

In her heart, she wants to see
her mother and native place again,
So carefree and frolic with childhood friends.

An image comes to appear in her mind,
She, holding with her mother hand,
Proudly she was walking down the market street.

People were shouting, cheering at her,
She felt happy, satisfied and overjoyed,
Being proud to be her mother's daughter.

She could tell to everyone
That the beautiful and gracious woman was her mother,
Who had got long ebony coconut oily black hair,

Wearing botches of Thanakkhar on both of her pouty cheeks,
Beautiful eyes like Myanmar movie star Khin Than Nu,
Walking as modest as a typical Myanmar woman should be.

Her mother embraced her tenderly,
Bought an adorable Myanmar doll on her 11th birthday,
Making a wishful wish for her.

"Be as beautiful as a princess,
Be as bright as a scholar,
Be as brave as the Lady."

The girl smiled at her mother,
Who smiled down at her, in turn,
Inside both of their hearts,

A warm sensation was brewing,
As strong as mother and daughter's love
Is binding together,

At this instant, future seems bright,
Bountiful, and promising,
With their love, and with their sincere hearts.

She looks back again at the River,
Which lays calm in the Yangon urban twilight,
*Phew!!!*She let her mind drifting with its flow.

Note:

Khin Than Nu– A renowned Burmese actress who was the apple of her audience in 1960 and 70's, when she starred in many good Burmese movies. Her fame is still going up to now.

Thanakkahar– A natural Burmese cosmetic which is used for protecting sun and beautifying one's self. It has got soothing and cool sensation when one applies its paste on cheeks.

Yangon– former capital of Myanmar/Burma

37. FEAR OF LOSS

Loss is a kind of fear
People incur it in their minds.
Because of that, they do
Unfair things.
When loss prevails,
Unhappiness one will land on.
But, it's a kind of world occurrences,
It will be a loss or a gain.
If you know the nature,
You will have no fear of loss.
Because even time is changing,
Summer to Rainy season
To winter again,
Be it you like it or not.
So, do not fear at all.

38. AN EGOCENTRIC BOSOM OF DESERT

It's hot,
Whenever it feels.
Even hot wind
Blows.
Fear, despair and loss
Burn in heart.
It is egocentric
Bosom of desert.
    No trees,
    No flowers,
    No streams,
No birds singing,
No greeneries,
No butterflies.

39. A REMEDY TO AN EGOCENTRIC BOSOM OF DESRT

Sprinkle water
To cool everything down.
    No heat,
    No loneliness,
    No fear,
    No hunger,
All will be disappeared at all.
Nurture kindess,
Love, compassion,
Then, it will turn into
A beautiful bed of grass.
Flowers will bloom,
Streams will laugh,
Butterflies will dance,
Deer will be frolic,
Children will play.

40. BULLET-1

Bang! *Whoosh…*
Hit.
Bang! Bang! *Whoosh…*
Hit.
Bang! Bang! Bang! *Whoosh…*
Hit.

All crows, mynas, sparrows suddenly flied off from their rest,
On the branches and twigs of big banyan trees,
Cawing loudly and desperately, showing all despairs,
Hovering and loitering around their site,
Not showing any desire to leave their place,
Horrendous time and experiences for them like a doom.

Another bang! and another *Whoosh…*
Total suppressed silence prevailed.
Not even a single crack of twig, even a stirring of leaves,
Everything stood still, no one could see in the street.
Deserted, scattered flip-flops, shoes, bricks, bits of bottles,
A total sight of mess; overwhelmed.

41. BULLET-2

Bullet is not flower;
There is no flagrance,
no beauty,
no sensation,
especially, not for decorations,
A sign of death, or a token of destruction.
Isn't it for protection?
or defending?
or violation?
Pressing the trigger doesn't tell
What is right or what is wrong.
It bangs instantly on firing,
Swifter than the speed of sound,
Harder than the hardest diamond,
Hit the spot with a definite force,
Leaving an inerasable and permanent hole.

42. YANGON CITY

The morning hums its harmony
Into the ajar door of the slumbering Yangon city,
Oh! Wake up Yangonite!
Which begins to sing its own song,
Together with chirpings of sparrows
And with cawl of crow.
It grows trees,
Still striving, and resisting every heat,
The weather and the engines make.
Forever enjoying by being called, "the Green City".
The city stirring, people out of the bed,
Each street of its own business is vibrating,
The full picture is sculpted.
The city looks at the people enthusiasts,
Feeling pleasant at its heart,
If they live happily,
If they work properly,
If they're engaged honestly,
If they're prospering.
It does not expect other things,
From them, for their offspring,
From their friends, from their colleagues,
From their bosses, from their rivals.
Only hope, hospitality, expectations, excellency
And future.

Cos' it nutures them, it takes good care of them,
It provides space for them, it gives chances for them,
To live a life, to earn a living, to value an urban life.
(It is like their parents,
They are like its offspring, O City!)
Enjoyment and engagement,
Safe and security,
Pride and Prosperity,
In the warm lap of the city, Yangon.

43. LONELINESS

You feel lonely,
When there is no one around you.

How can one face such situation?
Sometimes, one thinks it's unfair.

Actually, it is ugly.

Is there a law to be lonesome?
But, everyone knows loneliness is destitute.

It's dry, disoriented, disheveled.

So, try to harmonize with others.
Less agony, much company,
One will feel and face.

44. A JUMP

Jumping into the blue sea,
Without caring anything,
To have fun, and happiness,
That's his dream.

He is daring enough,
To jump off the cliff,
Who will take such a risk,
Only the strong man can do it.

The sea seems to embrace,
Such a brave one,
In its wavy blossom,
With much glee.

Any free-will swimmer can feel,
The sensation of liberty,
Of swimming in the ocean,
That's the eternity.

45. FEAR-1

Laughter…
Inaudible, at first,
Dry and hollow;
Coming in from afar.
Rolling in, rushing in,
With much force,
Like a tornado,
Or like a typhoon.
Menacing one's life,
Shaking one's life a lot,
Being hard to stay stable,
Wanting to outcry.
Stuck, speechless,
Motionless, petrified,
At the touch of fear.

46. FEAR-2

Grasped with icy hands,
Squeezed tight,
There's no sign of letting loose.
Staying inside,
Daring not to come out,
To face the truth and reality.
Losing one's rights,
To bring out one's might,
Fear must be gotten rid of,
From one's mind and life.

47. TO THE MAN WHO LIVED IN 29TH STREET

He who loved Yangon streets, not because Fraser's city's plan,
Nor Lord Dalhousie's dreams; simply, he fell in love with the cosmopolitan city.

What he found in it was amazing, he said to his best friend,
That there are treasures hidden in these streets,

Digging those up when he had a chance.

Among other things, authors like Rudyard Kipling,
George Orwell, Pablo Neruda, Paul Theroux, Ludu Sein Win, and Aung Cheit

Inspired him greatly while he was living in Yangon.
He really loved the literary life, and being an author,

He even managed to finish his doctorate in creative writing.
He walked freely in the maze of streets, wide and small,

Slinging his red bag on his left shoulder, with his panama hat,

His Apple laptop and quick-to-smile expression,

Making friends with locals, no discrimination towards age or gender,
He loved chatting, joking, philosophizing, and venturing,

A true global citizen and down-to-earth personality.

In his neighborhood in 29th street, he was known as "Mr Bob",
And well-liked by his friends and peers, showing their willingness,

And comfort in his association; they saw humour in him, and a quick wit,
He made their existence more meaningful and strengthened their identity,

To them, he was a sensible, true man.

Among his fascinations were Art House movies,
Also, Raymond Carver's books; he had a liking for old books,

Postcards, and posters which he managed to revive again,
On the stagnant walls of residents, expats and locals alike,

With his creative sense, and human touch.

Among his many success is "*Walking the Streets of Yangon*",
Which has become the Bible to those who like to explore the city's life,

He embossed his name in the city of Yangon, living fully in it,
Never wasting his time, always exploring and discovering,

He is remembered, not just on 29th Street, not just in Yangon.

Appendix

SHORT POEMS

Waves
Untied Existence
With or Without Reason
No More Belive in Myth
A Blank Heart
Aftermath
Algebra of Advice
A Bright Light
Only Then
A Chance to Choose
A Turn
The Light
Nature
Hope
Resilience
Advice
Cookies
My Lamp
Freedom
A New Form of Relationship
In Equal State
A Choice
A New Start
True Love

Silence
A Sincere Wish
Joe's Story
No Applause, Please
The Act of Washing Up
To the Goal

LONG POEMS
Animation Poem
Failure
Untitled Life
Urban Features
Right Answer
Mum's Girl
Fear of Loss
An Egocentric Bosom of Desert
A Remedy to an Egocentric Bosom of Desert
Bullet-1
Bullet-2
Yangon City
Loneliness
A Jump
Fear-1
Fear-2
To the Man who Lived in 29th Street

Notes

To my parents and teachers, late Dr. Bob Percival and those whose muses are wandering

www.ingramcontent.com/pod-product-compliance
Lightning Source LLC
LaVergne TN
LVHW050421160726
843469LV00041B/1171

* 9 7 8 9 3 5 4 5 8 4 4 9 7 *